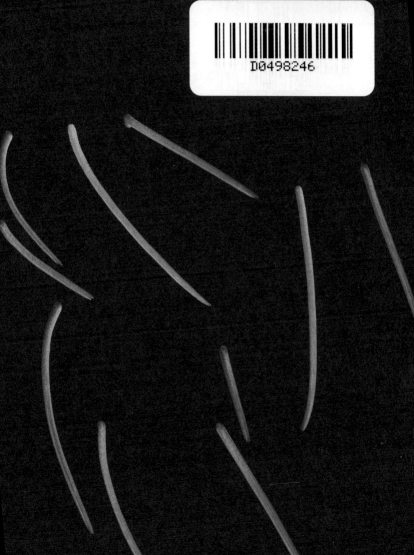

Spenser's Boston

PHOTOGRAPHS BY

KASHO KUMAGAI

ROBERT B. PARKER

Otto Penzler Books
New York

Otto Penzler Books
129 West 56th Street
New York, NY 10019
(Editorial Offices only)

Simon & Schuster Inc.
Rockefeller Center
1230 Avenue of the Americas
New York, NY 10020

English text copyright © 1994 by Robert B. Parker
Text copyright © 1988 by Robert B. Parker
Photographs copyright © 1989 by Kasho Kumagai
Originally published in 1989 in Japan by Hayakawa Publishing, Inc., Tokyo.
This book is published in 1994 by Otto Penzler Books by arrangement with
Hayakawa Publishing, Inc., Tokyo.

Manufactured in the United States of America

10   9   8   7   6   5   4   3   2   1

Library of Congress Cataloging-in-Publication Data
Parker, Robert B., date.
    Spenser's Boston / Robert B. Parker; photographs by Kasho Kumagai.
    p.   cm.
    1. Spenser (Fictitious character)   2. Literary landmarks—
Massachusetts—Boston.   3. Boston (Mass.)—Description and travel.
  I. Title.
  PS3566.A686S6   1994
  813′.54—dc20   94-17814   CIP

ISBN 1-883402-50-6

We went down along the Charles on Memorial Drive and across the Mass Ave bridge. Boston always looks great from there. Especially at night with the lights and the skyline against the starry sky and the sweep of the river in a graceful curve down toward the harbor.

—The Godwulf Manuscript

contents

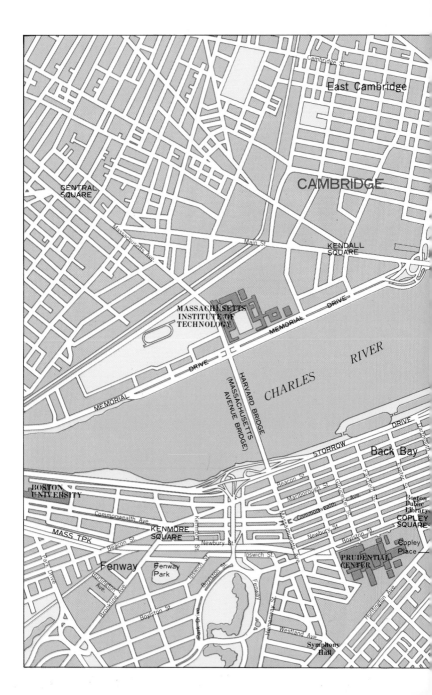

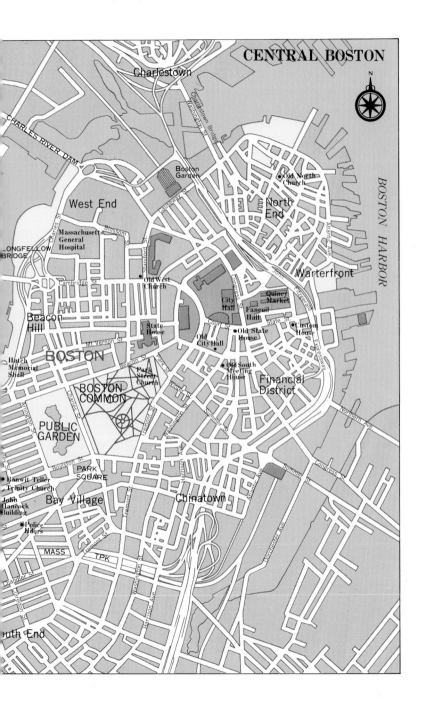

CENTRAL BOSTON

N

Charlestown

CHARLES RIVER DAM

Charlestown Bridge

Washington St

West End

Boston
Garden

LONGFELLOW
BRIDGE

Charles St

Massachusetts
General
Hospital

Blossom

Stanford St

Cambridge St

Old West
Church

Old North
Church

North
End

BOSTON HARBOR

Atlantic Ave

Waterfront

John F. Fitzgerald Expressway

Congress St

Quincy
Market

City
Hall

Faneuil
Hall

Custom
House

Beacon
Hill

Mt. Vernon St

State
House

Court St

State St

Old State
House

Hatch
Memorial
Shell

BOSTON

Beacon St

Park St

Old
City Hall

Old South
Meeting
House

Financial
District

Expressway

Charles St

BOSTON
COMMON

Park
Street
Church

Tremont St

Winter St

Washington St

Summer St

PUBLIC
GARDEN

Arlington St

Sumner St

Congress St

Northern Ave

Boylston St

Bonwit Teller
Trinity Church

John
Hancock
Building

PARK
SQUARE

Bay Village

Charles St

Tremont St

Washington St

Eliot St

Chinatown

Atlantic Ave

Dorchester Ave

Sumner St

Police
Hdqrs

MASS

Tremont St

TPK

Washington St

Harrison Ave

Chandler St

Clarendon St

outh End

"Name's Spenser with an *S*, like the poet. I'm in the Boston book. Under Tough."

Early Autumn

John Hancock Building

Marlborough St.

Beacon Hill

Fenway Park

Lynnfield

Charles River

J.J. Donovan's Tavern

Cape Cod

Arlington St.

Newbury St.

Spenser's Boston

BY ROBERT B. PARKER

*S*usan and Rachel Wallace and I were walking on a pleasant Saturday morning down Garden Street, toward Harvard Square. I had spent the night with both of them in Susan's place on Linnaean Street, though in truth I had spent more of the night with Susan than with Rachel Wallace; Susan being my sweet patootie and Rachel Wallace being a lesbian. I had been Rachel Wallace's bodyguard seven or eight years back when she was writing a book that proved troublesome to a lot of people, and now and then, when she came to Boston, she stopped by and slept on the hide-a-bed in Susan's living room, and we ate dinner and drank a little and talked about exciting things like clothes and makeup and sexual politics. Neither of them gave a rat's ass about the infield fly rule, and they both paid me no heed when I demonstrated that I could still do a one-arm push-up.

So I was sitting quietly with maybe my fifth beer and considering whether I should quit drinking when Rachel Wallace said, "I'd like to go sightseeing tomorrow."

Susan said, "What fun."

Rachel Wallace said, "I've been to Boston maybe fifteen times. I know Logan Airport, the Ritz Hotel, ten book-stores, and the major television stations."

"We'll take you tomorrow," Susan said. As she always did, she entered upon a new idea with full enthusiasm, her mind turning over the possibilities. She had on white shorts and a black sleeveless top and she sat on her ivory-covered sofa with her legs tucked under her as she often did.

"We'll take the T," she said. "Himself here knows more about Boston than John Winthrop."

"And," I said, "I'm alive."

Which was why we were walking down Garden Street on a pleasant Saturday morning heading toward Harvard Square.

"Cambridge is not," Rachel Wallace said, "technically part of Boston."

She always asked questions like that, by making an authoritative statement which you could correct if it were wrong. Most of the time it wasn't.

"That's right," I said. "There are those who say that, technically, Cambridge is not part of this world."

We walked past Cambridge Common, where Washington had formed his troops during the early stages of the Revolution, and on our side of Garden Street, the old church where he had set up headquarters. We turned down Appian Way past the Gutman Library, part of Harvard's system, and joined Brattle Street opposite the Loeb Theater.

"Harvard owns that, too," Susan said. "In fact, Harvard owns almost everything in Cambridge but me."

"The American Repertory Theatre," Rachel Wallace said. "The finest in the country."

"Yes," Susan said, "very *avant garde*."

"Do you go?" Rachel Wallace said to me.

"I have gone," I said. "But I get confused."

"There has to be a better place for theater to grow and

evolve," Rachel Wallace said.

"Yeah," I said, "that's what Paul Giacomin says. But he says I don't have to watch it. He says it'll go on okay without me."

Half a block past the Loeb Theater was the old Design Research building.

"Down there at the back," I said, "is the Harvest, the official Harvard Square restaurant and bar."

"We eat there several nights a week," Susan said. "And it has a take-out shop."

"When Susan bought the place on Linnaean Street," I said, "she asked if they could tear down the kitchen. They said it was a code violation."

"If you use a stove," Susan said, "it gets icky, and then you have to wash it."

"Exactly," Rachel Wallace said.

We followed the curve of Brattle Street through Brattle Square and up Elliot Street. To Harvard Square with the out-of-print bookstore in the center and the red brick of Harvard and the seclusion of Harvard Yard across Mass Avenue. There were shops and restaurants and bookstores and street musicians beginning to gather. At the

Red Line subway station in the square a group of funny-looking kids in leather and odd haircuts were sitting around behind the kiosk.

"This is the official counterculture headquarters," I said. "The look changes every few years, but this is where you come if you want to dress funny, and glower."

"Are they dangerous?" Rachel Wallace said.

"Only if you're allergic to bad breath," I said.

The Harvard Square subway station is nearly brand new. It is large, bright, clearly marked, and not unpleasant. The trains are slick-looking and clean as well. People who ride subways in New York or other parts of Boston are always puzzled by the Red Line.

We rode under Mass Ave, stopping at Central Square and then at Kendall. Those getting on and off at Central Square were mostly ethnic. Those getting on and off at Kendall were mostly WASPs with plastic pencil holders in their shirt pockets.

"What's in Kendall Square?" Rachel Wallace said.

"MIT," Susan said.

"And Michela's," I said.

"MIT, I know," Rachel Wallace said. "What's Michela's?"

"A grand Italian restaurant," Susan said.

"With a liquor license," I said.

Rachel nodded at me. "He likes it, doesn't he?" she said.

The train came up out of Kendall Square and onto the Longfellow Bridge, one of my favorite moments. You arched over the Charles with the gold dome of the State House on top of Beacon Hill in front of you, the Back Bay swept down to the right along the far bank of the Charles, and to the left, the estuary, the dam, and beyond, the harbor. There were a lot of small boats on the river, scutting along at a heel before the flukey off-shore breezes. The Longfellow Bridge itself, flashing past outside the train windows, was built in an era when bridges were supposed to look good as well as span a space. This one was built of gray stone and punctuated with massive gray towers. The train was in the center and traffic went past on either side.

We slowed as we approached Charles Street, and when the train stopped we got off. In back of us was the Charles Street Jail which, massively built of stone, and domed, looked like a jail ought to, and was considered obsolete. Next to it was Massachusetts General Hospital which, from this angle, did not look like a world-class hospital, which it was. Some architect had designed an addition to one of the buildings that sat on visible pilings atop the preexistent structure so that the whole thing looked like it had been propped up with two-by-fours until the carpenter could get to fixing it.

The Charles Street MBTA station is still elevated, and you cross the circle at Charles and Cambridge Streets on a footbridge, with the traffic snarling below.

Susan was walking ahead of me wearing tight jonquil-colored pants and a lavender blouse. She'd been doing two aerobics classes a day for the last couple of years and her backside looked as tight and curvesome as it probably had when she was twenty. I admired it, feeling a little guilty in Rachel Wallace's company, wondering if she could detect sexism on some nonverbal plane I didn't know about. Actually Rachel Wallace's backside wasn't too bad, either, but I figured that it was pushing my luck to admire hers.

As we started up Charles Street, Rachel Wallace said, "Oh my God, is this Boston or what?"

The dominance of red brick and two- and three-story colonial design made the whole street look like something out of *Make Way for Ducklings*. To the left, Beacon Hill spread level to the river. In the nineteenth century the

Charles River mingled with the harbor and lapped at the very edges of Charles Street until the top of Beacon Hill was lowered by carting the dirt from the top and filling in the so-called Back Bay. The area west of Charles Street is still called Back Bay and, unlike the rest of the city, is flat as a table top and arranged in a grid pattern with the cross streets named alphabetically from Arlington to Ipswich, although Mass Avenue and the Mass Turnpike Extension have isolated Ipswich Street from the rest of Back Bay and people sort of forget about it.

"Over there," I said, "is Toscano, one of the best restaurants in the city—Italian food to rival Michela's."

"Spaghetti and meatballs with tomato sauce and pre-grated Parmesan cheese?" Rachel Wallace said.

"If you said that in Toscano," I said, "or for that matter, Michela's, I would be forced to prevent them from assaulting you."

"You've done that duty before," Rachel Wallace said. "I must say you do it well."

"Thanks," I said.

"If rather noisily."

I heard Susan chuckle.

"It is unbecoming of a woman to chuckle," I said.

"Really?" Rachel Wallace said.

"He thinks women shouldn't whistle, either," Susan said.

The two women laughed.

"What is life without rules?" I said.

"Pleasant," Susan said, but I knew she didn't mean it.

"Let's look at Beacon Hill, a little," Rachel Wallace said.

"Louisburg Square," Susan said. "It is the essence of Beacon Hill and of Old Boston."

We went up the narrow streets for a couple of blocks, with the narrow four-story red brick townhouses crowding the sidewalk, and turned into Louisburg Square. There was a small grassy plot in the center. The plot was ringed with wrought iron railings, and there were many signs warning that one shouldn't park in Louisburg Square inasmuch as it was private and belonged only to people who lived there and we weren't any of them. At the Mount Vernon end was a statue of Aristides; at the Pinckney Street end was a statue of Columbus. Probably the only two foreign-sounding names ever to invade Louisburg Square.

"There's no one in sight," Rachel Wallace said.

"They're inside," I said, "reading Cotton Mather."

We walked back down the hill on Pinckney Street, turned left on Charles and continued along to Beacon Street. Before us was the Public Garden to the right and the Common to our left. We crossed and walked through the garden.

"There is also a basketball arena called the Garden, isn't there?" Rachel Wallace said.

"Boston Garden," I said. "Singular, as is the Public Garden. Boston Common is also singular. Hayshakers from New York and Los Angeles are always looking ignorant by saying Boston Gardens and Boston Commons, and generally disgracing themselves in front of us Beantown sophisticates."

"Yes," Rachel Wallace said.

We cut across the Public Garden, past the statues of a mother duck and a string of ducklings, based on the famous children's story. Ahead was the lagoon where the Swan Boats cruised, peddled by a summer vacation college kid in back, fronted by the jumbo swan replica in the prow. Couples and families with kids crowded onto the benches and fed peanuts to ducks so hip that they ignored shells from which the peanuts had been eaten. The Swan

Boat pond was pinched in the middle like Lillian Russell, and across the pinch was a miniature suspension bridge. We crossed it.

"Is this bridge based on a real one somewhere?" Rachel Wallace asked.

"Yes," Susan said.

"Which one?"

"I don't know," Susan said positively.

We passed the monumentally scaled statue of George Washington on horseback, erect in the saddle, staring heroically down the Commonwealth Avenue mall at the statue of William Lloyd Garrison, and beyond.

There were statues in the mall all the way down Commonwealth.

"It looks like an avenue in Paris," Rachel Wallace said.

"*Oui,*" I said. "*C'est vrai.*"

"Multilingual," Susan said.

"*Si, señorita,*" I said.

Susan looked at Rachel Wallace. "He is an excellent argument for lesbianism, I must say."

"It's probably not a condition to be argued," Rachel Wallace said.

"True," Susan said.

"Next time I give a tour," I said, "I'm going to ask Hawk to come. He respects a man's linguistic range."

"Hawk actually *speaks* French, cutie, and understands it," Susan said.

"Does he really?" Rachel Wallace said.

"Oui," I said. *"C'est vrai."*

We walked past the Ritz.

The doorman said, "Hello, Ms. Wallace."

She said, "Hello, Frank. What time is it?"

He looked at his watch.

"12:02," he said.

"Well, then," Rachel Wallace said. "It is time."

The doorman smiled. "Yes, ma'am," he said, and gave the revolving door a small shove and Rachel Wallace headed into the Ritz. Susan and I went after her.

They've redone the Ritz bar and now it looks more like all the other bars in all the other hotels in the Occident, but it still offers a lovely view and a grand martini.

"It is incredible," Susan said as the maitre d' seated us by the window, "that you are actually wearing a tie."

"And jacket," I said, "and not jeans. I figured she'd lead us here before the day ended."

"Semper paratus," Susan murmured and put her hand on top of mine.

"Will it be the usual, Ms. Wallace?" the maitre d' asked.

The Ritz does not serve a double martini, but if you want one it will make two singles in little carafes and serve the second as soon as you have finished the first. It was, for Rachel Wallace, *the usual.* Susan ordered a Perrier and I ordered one too.

Rachel Wallace raised her eyebrows.

"Age," I said. "One beer in midday and I tend to need a nap."

"I don't like that," Rachel Wallace said. "It is frightening to see mortality edge in on the man of steel."

"I am still more powerful than a locomotive," I said. "And a sexual athlete."

Susan gazed thoughtfully out the window, across Arlington Street at the Public Garden.

"Promises," she said, "promises." And her big dark eyes glimmered.

Rachel Wallace drank her martini. Susan drank half of her Perrier, and I had three. Then I paid the bill and we strolled up Newbury Street.

Newbury Street is as close as Boston gets to Rodeo Drive, a half-mile or so of boutiques and antique shops and stores that I'd never been in but had leaned against the outside for long periods while Susan plumbed them to their very souls.

"We'd better do a swoop through here," Susan said.

"Look at that skirt," Rachel Wallace said.

"I feel it is unbecoming to a feminist to demean her species through stereotypically girlish behavior."

"Like shopping?" Susan said.

"Perhaps," I said.

"Keeps me in touch with my roots," Rachel Wallace said, and they went into the shop and I leaned against the marble surface to the left of the front door. Across the way was an art gallery where Susan and I had bought one of the limited edition Michael Delacroix prints for Susan's living room after she'd moved to Cambridge. Cars cruised slowly, looking for parking spaces and never finding any. Parking in Boston is something that you never see done. There are cars parked on either side of Newbury Street, for instance. But you never know who did it. The buildings, three, four, occasionally five stories high, offered a lovely jumble of shapes against the high sky. Except in the heart of downtown, Boston, like San Francisco, has rather low architecture and one is often aware of the sky. Two young men were playing frisbee with a black lab wearing a red kerchief instead of a dog collar, the lab dashing in among shoppers and parked cars to nab the frisbee in mid flight. There were roller skaters and skateboarders and many young couples from the suburbs strolling up and down Newbury Street, stopping at one of many outdoor cafés, having white wine and strawberry daiquiris and Sam Adams beer, eating cheeseburgers and spinach salads. In amongst the suburbanites, sleeker, more *au courant,* and a little haughtier, were many of the young urban professionals for whom Newbury Street was the corner on which they hung.

I shifted a little against the marble. The gun on my hip was digging into me a little. I'd have to learn to wear it farther forward if I were going to do a lot of leaning.

A young woman passed me wearing very tight blue jeans and red shoes with three-inch heels that caused her to walk with a significant hip sway. As I watched her walk down the street Susan and Rachel Wallace came out of the shop with several plastic shopping bags.

"Is that woman a suspect in a felony?" Susan said.

"No, I was just speculating on whether there is any room inside those jeans for an undergarment of any sort."

"No," Susan said, "there isn't."

"I thought not," I said.

"Since you now have the answer to your inquiry," Susan said, "why are you still staring at her?"

"I was hoping she might drop a card bearing her phone number," I said.

"Should she do so," Rachel Wallace said, "perhaps you could pass it along to me when you're through."

We had lunch at a café called Dartmouth Street where Rachel Wallace had another double martini and Susan and I switched to San Pellegrino water. After lunch we strolled up to Copley Place.

If you were from Houston and staying in Boston and felt homesick you could go to Copley Place. It is a two-story shopping mall that looks like the Galleria in Houston, or, for that matter, the Beverly Center in Los Angeles and Water Tower Place in Chicago, and almost every other recent urban shopping mall in the United States. It was full of marble and expensive shops and a waterfall and several restaurants, and anonymity. If you were from anyplace and homesick, you could go to Copley Place and feel at home, or at somebody else's home. Set atop a huge underground garage, and anchored at either end by large chain hotels, Copley Place was set up so that if you came to Boston and didn't like it you'd never have to see it. You could stay right inside. And sleep and eat and drink and shop and go home and tell the gang that Boston seemed pretty bland to you.

Susan and Rachel Wallace were able to find several things to buy in Copley Place and I found several places to lean and observe while they did it.

Back out in Copley Square we passed the lovely former front of the Boston Public Library. A new addition had been tagged onto the other side of the building and the grand entrance was now a side entrance and a place where many street people congregated to drink from brown paper bags or munch a Twinkie that someone had thrown away half-eaten. Across the way the square was being recreated after the unfortunate experiment in urban depression which had endured there for some years.

"What is that lovely church?" Rachel Wallace said as we turned down Boylston Street.

"Trinity Church," I said. "H. H. Richardson did it. The one back there, too, on Boylston, the Old South Church."

Trinity was cut stone and pillars and looked everything a famous church ought to look. Next to it the burnished glass facade of the fifty-two-story John Hancock Building reflected the square surprisingly well.

"Top of the Hancock," I said to Rachel Wallace, "is a grand panorama of the city."

"Let's skip it," Rachel said.

"I thought you were a tourist," I said.

"No. I'm visiting friends," she said. "That is entirely different."

"Of course," I said.

Much of Boylston Street was in the hubbub of restoration, rebuilding, and new construction. Susan reached out and took my hand as we walked.

We passed my office building at the corner of Berkeley and Boylston, above the Boston Five Cent Savings Bank.

"I may have to move," I said. "They are threatening to rehab me again."

"As long as I know where to find you," Rachel Wallace said.

She always amazed me. I'd watched her drink two double martinis and she was as sober and lucid as Susan and I who had drunk two glasses of soda water . . . maybe more lucid than I.

We passed the new Four Seasons Hotel on Boylston and crossed at Charles Street again to cut across the Common.

"Why Common?" Rachel Wallace said.

"Because it was once common grazing area for cattle," Susan said. "In the seventeenth century."

Beacon Hill rose to the left of the Common as we followed the long walk past the Soldiers and Sailors Monument heading toward Tremont Street. Beacon Street ran up the hill parallel to our course. At the top of Beacon Hill, the State House stood with its golden dome and Bulfinch front glittering in the afternoon sunlight. Park Street came down at right angles from Beacon to Tremont. At the corner stood Park Street Church.

"Brimstone Corner," Susan was saying, "because during the revolution the Colonial army stored gunpowder in the church."

We crossed Tremont Street—so named because there were once three hills in Boston on which the city had been originally built—near the entrance to the Park Street subway station, which is the main station in the city, and walked down Winter Street past the Locke-Ober Café.

We stopped and looked in at the dark wood and polished coffee urns and the Victorian-looking nude under which various well-known Bostonians have elected to sit. The waiters wore tuxedos.

"Men only until maybe fifteen years ago," I said to Rachel Wallace, "in the, ah, so-called men's bar."

"I recall you telling me that story," she said. "I believe there was an exchange with a priest."

"Indeed," I said.

At the foot of Winter Street, Washington Street crosses, and we strolled along it through Downtown Crossing where there was always music and street vendors and the two giants of Boston retailing, Jordan Marsh and Filene's, stood right across the street from one another. Traffic was banned from this part of Washington Street and the people crowded sidewalks and streets equally. This was less chichi than the Back Bay. This was verging on downtown and there were Burger Kings instead of outdoor cafés and croissant shops. We passed the Old South Meeting House, and the Old State House, and turned onto City Hall Plaza where the new city hall loomed like a kind of oversized red brick Stonehenge in a sea of unused red brick plaza where, in winter, the wind blew through as it is said to do on the steppes of Russia. We went down the stairs beside City Hall and across the street to Quincy Market, the first and still the best of the restored marketplaces. It was filled, as it nearly always was, with people eating from the thirty or so food stalls in the central market, sitting at outdoor tables in front of one or another of the restaurants, buying from the myriad boutiques in the north and south market buildings, and browsing through the newly completed addition at the waterfront end of the market area where the Sharper Image sold expensive things that had no use to people who willingly waited in line to buy them.

Then we were at the harbor. There's very little warning in Boston when you hit the water. You are strolling along on a congested street in the heart of the financial district and you cross a wide road and there's the water. There are no transitional warehouses, or boatyards, or places that sell fish and have lobster pots outside. Most of the heavy harbor work, boats docking and loading and unloading, that stuff, is done on either side of the central Boston waterfront, in South Boston and East Boston and Charlestown, in terminals along the mouth of the Mystic River, and in oil storage facilities up Chelsea Creek a ways. The piers along the downtown waterfront are mostly devoted to restaurants, condominiums and hotels. The aquarium is there, a still, wet, curving space with a central tank several stories high around which the viewing walks curve like a spiral staircase. And the New Boston Hotel, where we ended up going in for a drink before dinner.

Settled into their lounge, with a view of the harbor and the wonderful pagoda they had built at water's edge, anticipating a large dinner in a while, I indulged in a Sam Adams beer while Rachel Wallace had her usual, and Susan sipped a Ramos Fizz.

"You didn't see Fenway Park," I said, "and you should have; but some among us are very surly about baseball."

Susan rolled her eyes over the foamy top of her fizz.

"And you didn't see Boston Garden for a similar reason," I said. "But this was a pretty good one-day look at the town."

"It was grand," Rachel Wallace said. She ate an olive off the little plastic spear that they had mounted it on when they stuck it in her martini. "There are very few unattractive places in Boston."

"There are a few," I said, "but we steered around them."

"Did I miss many tourist attractions?"

"All of them," Susan said. There was a tiny speck of foam from her Ramos Fizz on the tip of her nose. I reached over and brushed it off. She patted my thigh. "Old Ironsides, Bunker Hill Monument, the hall of flags in the State House, Paul Revere's house, and that's without even getting out to the suburbs."

"If we went to the suburbs," I said, "we could miss the Minuteman statue, the Buckman Tavern, the Rude Bridge that arched the flood, Plimoth Plantation . . . the stuff that dreams are made of."

"We can miss those tomorrow, too," Rachel Wallace said, and drank most of her martini. Later we took a cab back to Cambridge and Susan changed, although she already looked better than Ivana Trump, and the three of us went down to Rarities restaurant in the Charles Hotel and had a nearly perfect meal.

SUMMER

Charles River

Old State House

Trinity Church

Charles River

Beacon Hill

Harvard Univ.

Cambridge

I weigh one-ninety-five, I can bench-press three hundred pounds. I used to be a fighter. And I scuffle for a living.

Promised Land

Massachusetts Ave. Bridge

Cambridge

"Were you not a good fighter?"

"I was good. I was not great. Being a good fighter is no life. Only great ones lead a life worth too much."

Looking for Rachel Wallace

"You want to help people."

"Yes."

"Why?"

"Makes me feel good," I said.

A Savage Place

Cambridge

Fenway Park

Locke-Ober Café

Quincy Market

Newbury St.

"We know what hurts," I said, "and what doesn't. We know about being scared and being brave."

Looking for Rachel Wallace

"Don't quit," I said. "You want something, you go after it. I was nearly thirty-five before I could get in with the wrong crowd."

The Widening Gyre

Fenway Park

Public Garden

Boston Common

"Couch or floor," I said.

"The rug is thick."

"Floor it is," I said, and put my arms around her. Both towels slipped to the floor. With her mouth against mine Susan said, "No missionary position, big fella. The rug's not that soft."

"Neither am I."

"Elegant," she murmured. "Positively ritzy."

Ceremony

Public Garden

Washington St.

Charles River

Massachusetts Ave.

Northern Ave.

Smith & Wesson

I told her about the job.

"Bounty hunter," she said.

"Yeah, I guess so. Just like the movies."

The Judas Goat

Berkeley St.

"I hear you were a pretty good cop before you got fired. What'd you get fired for?"

"Insubordination. It's one of my best things."

The Godwulf Manuscript

Route 1A

Combat Zone

Ritz Carlton Hotel

"Nice day," Susan murmured.

"For some," I said.

"Not for most?"

"Pretty to think so," I said.

Ceremony

Copley Plaza Hotel

AUTUMN

Public Garden

Commonwealth Ave.

Boylston St.

I moved down Boylston Street to the corner of Berkeley, second floor. I was half a block from Brooks Brothers and right over a bank. I felt at home. In the bank they did the same kind of stuff the fortune-teller and the bookie had done. But they dressed better.

Early Autumn

"Two hundred dollars a day," I said. "And expenses."

"Expenses?"

"Yeah, you know. Sometimes I run out of ammunition and have to buy more."

Looking for Rachel Wallace

Harvard Yard

Arlington St.

Marlborough St.

I said, "He and I
are part of the
same cold place.
You aren't. You're
the source of
warmth. Hawk has
none. You're what
makes me different
from Hawk."

Ceremony

Exeter St.

Back Bay

State House

Marlborough St.

Charles St.

State House

Marlborough St.

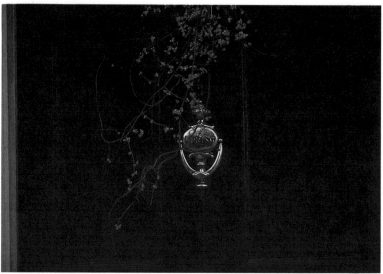

Beacon Hill

"That's the part that does matter. How? It's the only part that matters."

"Honor?" Susan said.

"Yeah," I said.

Mortal Stakes

Public Garden

"Nonsense, that's the machismo convention. It gets people killed and for what. Life isn't a John Wayne movie."

Promised Land

Stuart St.

Atlantic Ave.

Linnaean St.

Marlborough St.

"I'll teach him what I know. I know how to do carpentry. I know how to cook. I know how to punch. I know how to act."

Early Autumn

Susan was quiet, looking down at me. "Spring will be a little late this year," she said.

"For Paul? Yeah." I laughed with no pleasure. "Spring is gone. It's early autumn for Paul. If I can do it."

"And if he can," Susan said.

Early Autumn

Boston Common

"I lost you for a couple of years back there," I said. "I found out that I could live without you. And I found out also that I didn't want to."

"Because?"

"Because I love you," I said. "Because you are in my life like the music at the edge of silence."

Crimson Joy

Susan smiled and shook her head. "Were you prepared to defend my virtue?"

"I'm in pursuit of it myself, and I don't like poachers."

God Save the Child

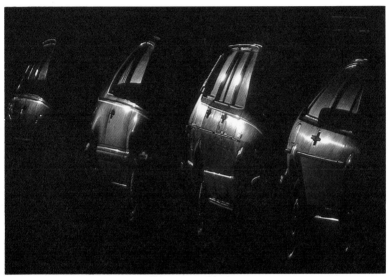

Commonwealth Ave.

Cambridge

Storrow Drive

Mystic River Bridge

Warren Tavern

Locke-Ober Café

It is Old Boston the way the Custom House tower is Old Boston. The decor is plain. The waiters wear tuxedos.

Looking for Rachel Wallace

Locke-Ober Café

Boylston St.

WINTER

Charles River

Charles River

Marlborough St.

Commonwealth Ave.

Arlington St.

"I'll tell you if you need to know it. I don't make a living telling cops everything they want to know about clients."

The Godwulf Manuscript

Marlborough St.

Marlborough St.

Beacon Hill

Arlington St.

"It's like us," she said.

"The champagne?"

"You have to pour it so carefully. It's like our lovemaking. Careful, gentle, delicate, being careful not to spill over."

A Catskill Eagle

I carried her through the living room and down the hall to her bedroom. It's not as easy as it looked in *Gone With the Wind*.

Crimson Joy

Beacon Hill

Ritz Bar

She said, "Come in, Mr. Spenser. I'm Susan Silverman," and came around the desk to shake hands.

Her breasts were good, her thighs were terrific. When she shook hands with me, I felt something click down back of my solar plexus.

I said hello without stammering and sat down.

God Save the Child

135

Pier 4

"He said girls cook."

"He was half right. Girls cook,
so do boys. So do women, so do
men."

Early Autumn

Cambridge

"You're quite thoughtful," she said,
"for a man your size."

"You never been my size," I
said. "You wouldn't understand."

A Savage Place

Tremont St.

Washington St.

Clarendon St.

Beacon St.

Commonwealth Ave.

Arlington St.

Mt. Vernon St.

Beacon St.

CROSSING
MYSTIC RIVER BRIDGE

Lynnfield

Lynnfield

Lynnfield Center

Lynnfield

Lynnfield

I drove past the old common, with its white church and meeting-house, and turned left down Main Street. I knew the way to Susan Silverman's house. She lived 100 yards up from the common in a small weathered shingle Cape with blue window boxes filled with red petunias.

Mortal Stakes

She put her face against my chest and we stood that way, wordless and still for a long time.

"For as long as we live," I said.

"Maybe longer," Susan said.

Promised Land

Lynnfield

Andover

"He'd like to be Sir Gawain. He was born five hundred years too late."

"Six hundred years," I said.

Looking for Rachel Wallace

"Okay, Jane Eyre, I got you."

Tears began to run down her face, and I put my arms around her, and she cried. And I cried. In between crying I said, "I got you. I got you."

Looking for Rachel Wallace

Lynnfield

Lynnfield

Rosalie's

Marblehead

Marblehead Harbor

108 MILES
TO CAPE COD

The whole Cape echoed with a sense of the ocean, not necessarily its sight and not always its scent or sound. Sometimes just the sense of vast space on each side of you. Of open brightness stretching a long way under the sun.

Promised Land

Cape Cod

Cape Cod

Cape Cod

Cape Cod

"Tell me about Spenser. Have you known him long?"

"I met him in 1973," Susan said, "but I've known him forever."

Looking for Rachel Wallace

Cape Cod

"We are able to love one another
with the intensity that we do because we are able to be separate
while we are at the same
time one."

Crimson Joy

Cape Cod

CAPE

Cape Cod

Living around Bos-
ton for a long time
you tend to think of
Cape Cod as the
promised land. Sea,
sun, sky, health,
ease, boisterous ca-
maraderie, a kind of
real-life beer
commercial.

Promised Land

Hyannis

Provincetown

Provincetown

Cape Cod

Cape Cod

Provincetown

Provincetown

Cape Cod

From my room at the Ritz-Carlton Hotel where I am presently staying, I have a good view of the city of Boston enveloped in the mists of a chilly winter's rain. There is the Public Garden, Boston Common, and the gold-domed State House, and immediately behind them the downtown section and its cluster of tall buildings. And there are rows of brick houses along the south side of Beacon Street, with chimneys of assorted shapes and sizes protruding from rooftops. In the distance, hazily, I can glimpse the Charles River, while directly in front of the hotel, Arlington and Boylston Streets stretch out toward the Combat Zone.

Through my window is seen the wide compass of "Spenser's landscape."

It was last winter that I first visited Ash Street, near Harvard Yard, and the home of Mr. Robert B. Parker. Mr. Parker greeted me with "Welcome to Spenser's rooms," and then he showed me the library.

Go to Boston! Perhaps I will even have a chance to meet "Spenser." These were my thoughts upon setting out for this city, and now I had had my first encounter with "Spenser."

The Common. Beacon Hill. Red Sox ballgames. Dining at the Locke-Ober Café. The Athletic Club and the Ritz Bar. . . . On each of my visits to Boston Mr. Parker accompanied me for picture-taking. I had imagined him as a hero, but there was a gentleness, despite the physical strength implicit in his broad shoulders, when he strolled the streets and boulevards of Boston, talking about his own hero like his closest friend. It made me feel as though Spenser in *Early Autumn* had indeed been my guide.

During my current visit I have met a number of remarkable people. I would particularly like to express thanks to Mr. Daniel Montague of the Massport Authority; Mr. Larry Meehan of the Boston Convention and Visitors Bureau; Mr. Jan Furutani of the Massachusetts Office of Travel and Tourism; and especially to Ms. Shoko Hirao of the Massport Authority and Peter Dale of DL Transnational Associates, Inc., all of whom rendered invaluable assistance.

I would also like to express my deep gratitude to Ms. Kayoko Inoue of Tsuru Enterprise Co., Ltd.; Mr. Akihiro Maruki, editor in chief of Hot Dog Press, Kodansha; art director Mr. Shigeru Yamaoka; Vice President Hiroshi Hayakawa of Hayakawa Publishing, Inc., and Mr. Kazuyoshi Sogawa, editor.

Finally, very special thanks to Mr. Robert B. Parker for giving me assistance on my photo-taking sessions, and to Ryu Murakami for accompanying me to Boston and for writing his message of endorsement.

Kasho Kumagai
Boston
February 1989

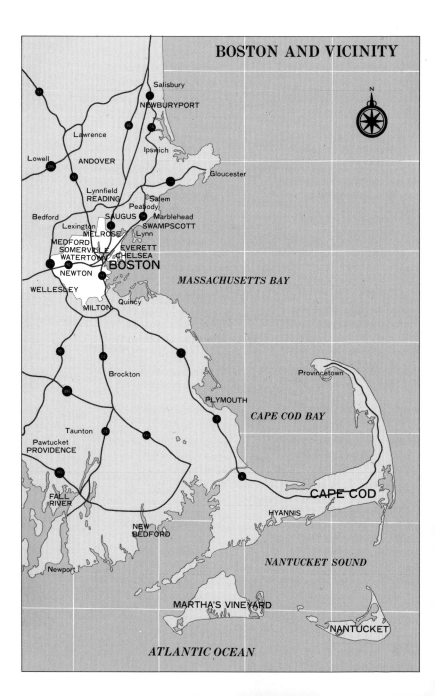

1. BUNKER HILL

This obelisk-shaped tower on the heights at Charlestown commemorates a major battle of the War of Independence. It is 67 meters (220 feet) tall. It marks the battle of June 17, 1775, when Americans engaged a numerically superior British force here, fighting literally down to their last bullet.

> I drove north out of Boston over the Mystic River Bridge with the top down on my car. On the right was Old Ironsides at berth in the Navy Yard and to the left of the bridge the Bunker Hill Monument.
>
> —*God Save the Child*

2. CONSTITUTION

This frigate, known as "Old Ironsides" from its sturdy oak construction, has been moored at the Navy Yard since it was refurbished. Launched at Boston in 1797, it was used to fight the British in the War of 1812. The ship served with distinction, never suffering defeat. It was refurbished from 1973 to 1975, and in its preserved state remains a vivid reminder of an important period in American history. It also lays claim to being the world's oldest warship still afloat.

3. PARK STREET CHURCH

Constructed in 1809 at the intersection of Park and Tremont Streets. The white steeple, retaining its original shape and design, typifies the architectural style of the period. It is well known as the site of William Lloyd Garrison's antislavery speech of 1829, and formerly was called "Brimstone Corner" for serving as a munitions store during the War of 1812.

4. STATE HOUSE

Occupying one corner of the old redbrick neighborhood of Beacon Hill, this "new" State House was constructed by the noted eighteenth-century architect Charles Bulfinch on the grounds of John Hancock's house. The gold dome makes it one of Boston's best-known landmarks.

> I always enjoyed a reason to go to the State House. The great gold dome gleamed in the summer sun and from the top of the steps you could look down across the Common and feel the density of the old city thickening behind you in time's corridor.
>
> —*Valediction*

5. QUINCY MARKET

Quincy Market is old and lovingly restored. Outside on either side are arcades with more stalls and terrace cafés, and in restored brick buildings parallel were clothing stores and specialty shops and restaurants. It claims to be the number-one tourist attrac-

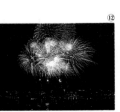

tion in Boston, and it should be. If you were with a girl in the market area, it would be hard not to hold hands with her. Jugglers and strolling musicians moved around the area. The market is never empty.

—*Looking for Rachel Wallace*

6. OLD STATE HOUSE

Situated at the intersection of Washington and State Streets. Built in 1712 as a parliament building for the colonial government. A spectator gallery was built in 1766, giving citizens their first opportunity to witness the functioning of government. The Declaration of Independence was read here to the assembled citizens of Boston. It currently serves as a historical museum, perserving many important documents from early American history.

7. HATCH MEMORIAL SHELL

An attractive outdoor concert area constructed some fifty years ago on the shores of the Charles River. City residents enjoy top-of-the-line entertainment here in a relaxed setting. Thanks to the support of Arthur Fiedler and the Boston Pops, it won fame as Boston's premiere place of entertainment.

At eight the next morning I was out jogging along the Charles. From the concert hall on the Esplanade to the BU Bridge was two miles, and I always tried to make the round trip in about forty minutes.

—God Save the Child

8. OLD CITY HALL

Situated on School Street, the Old City Hall is architecturally one of Boston's most beautiful buildings. At present this splendorous structure, built in the French Second Empire style, contains a number of offices and one of the city's most elegant French restaurants. In front of the Old City Hall is a statue of Boston-born Benjamin Franklin, whose parents are buried in the nearby Old Granary Burying Ground.

9. OLD NORTH CHURCH

Built in 1723 as "a place of worship for all the people," this church on Salem Street is well known by the name Christ Church. It is the oldest church in Boston and is still used as a place of worship. It is known as the church where lanterns were hung on April 18, 1775, to signal Paul Revere's famous ride to warn of a British attack.

Out to the right now was the harbor and the harbor islands and the long curving waterfront. The steeple of the Old North Church poked up among the warehouses and lofts.   —*God Save the Child*

10. MUSEUM OF FINE ARTS

Ranks as one of America's three leading art museums, together with New York's Metropolitan Museum of Art and the Art Institute of Chicago. Originally constructed at Copley Square in 1870, it grew rapidly and in 1909 was moved to the present Huntington Avenue site. Four buildings were added in 1981, and in 1983 an Asian Gallery was completed through a gift of $1.4 million from the Japanese government. This wing is noted for its Egyptian collection, but also has a splendid exhibit of Japanese articles, including 5,000 paintings, 6,000 prints, 7,700 ceramic articles, and 600 Japanese swords.

11. OLD SOUTH MEETING HOUSE

Ever since construction of this building on Milk Street in 1729 as a Puritan chapel, Bostonians have used it for important gatherings. Entering the building, one can look through a window on the right side and see Benjamin

Franklin's birthplace. Used as a meeting place by participants in the Boston Tea Party, the building is designated as a National Historic Landmark. Recently it has continued to play an important role as a location for public forums and educational programs.

12. CHARLES RIVER—JULY 4

The Boston Harborfest is the year's most colorful water event. The festival is climaxed with a traditional Independence Day concert at Hatch Memorial Shell, and from 8 to 10 P.M. a spectacular fireworks display is seen over the Charles River. More than 200,000 people line up along the bridge, go out on boats, or stroll along the many footpaths as the festival reaches a peak. Reservations for rooms with a view of the fireworks must be made months in advance.

Camera: Minolta 9000
Minolta 7700 i

Lens: 20mm, 24mm, 50mm, 85mm
MACRO 100mm, 200mm, 300mm, 600mm

Film: PKR, KR, Fuji 400, 1600, Try X

About the photographer

Kasho Kumagai
1944 Born in Fukuoka Prefecture.
1966 Graduated from Nihon University, Department of Fine Arts
(Photography).
Entered photography department of Associated Press, Tokyo
Bureau.

1968 Left AP.
Free-lance photographer.
Became member of Association of Japan Photographers.

1979 Published *Inshallah* (published by Kaze Shobo).
Photograph exhibition.

1985 Published *Natty Jamaica* (published by Kyuryu-Do).
Photograph exhibition.

1987 Photo exhibit, "Tropical Winds Collection."

Address: STUDIO FOCUS 21
1-2-9, Ohara, Setagayaku, Tokyo, Japan, 156
Tel: (03) 3485-4744